AF448394

Ake Selander has written this book as his memoir so that an allergy sufferer can compare the author's journey with their own.

This is dedicated to Eric Berne MD, who has given me most of his books. *What Do You Say After You Say Hello?* is important reading today. My sister was a nurse in Denver Colorado and met Berne many times.

Ake Selander

FOOD ALLERGY

New Information to Keep Healthy!

AUSTIN MACAULEY PUBLISHERS™

LONDON • CAMBRIDGE • NEW YORK • SHARJAH

Copyright © Ake Selander 2024

All rights reserved. No part of this publication may be reproduced, distributed, or transmitted in any form or by any means, including photocopying, recording, or other electronic or mechanical methods, without the prior written permission of the publisher, except in the case of brief quotations embodied in critical reviews and certain other non-commercial uses permitted by copyright law. For permission requests, write to the publisher.

Any person who commits any unauthorized act in relation to this publication may be liable to criminal prosecution and civil claims for damages.

All of the events in this memoir are true to the best of author's memory. The views expressed in this memoir are solely those of the author.

Ordering Information
Quantity sales: Special discounts are available on quantity purchases by corporations, associations, and others. For details, contact the publisher at the address below.

Publisher's Cataloging-in-Publication data
Selander, Ake
Food Allergy

ISBN 9798886930115 (Paperback)
ISBN 9798886930139 (ePub e-book)
ISBN 9798886930122 (Audiobook)

Library of Congress Control Number: 2023917931

www.austinmacauley.com/us

First Published 2024
Austin Macauley Publishers LLC
40 Wall Street, 33rd Floor, Suite 3302
New York, NY 10005
USA

mail-usa@austinmacauley.com
+1 (646) 5125767

Table of Contents

Preface

After I was tested at two different allergy laboratories and was found to be free from allergies, I wrote to the professor of allergies and stated that their allergy tests did not find any food allergy. I got no answer. I looked into all allergies and found that I was ninety-five percent free of allergy symptoms. I then sent an e-mail to the Minister for Health, asking to have a dialogue about problems related to food allergies. I said that I could save 10 to 15 million euros per year with my SUPER DIET. I was tested for two and a half years and no allergies were found. I searched the issue myself for six years and found almost all allergens, that make a person sick, were present in my food. The response from the female minister was diabolical, she replied stating that: Food Hypersensitivity is a well-known problem and she was glad that I had found all the allergens that made me sick. It was not a problem for the female health minister, and she thanked me for my e-mail, but why did she not ask about the 10 to 15 million euros?

First Symptom

When I was eleven or twelve years old, I went to an elementary school were one of the requirements was to perform a morning prayer. It was the school principal's turn to lead the prayer; it sometimes lasted over half an hour. I remember three students who passed-out because of what we had to endure. I also went to the deck once. It was due to the weakness of my food. Food was almost as bad just after the war as it was during the war. I also had problems with sweaty hands. The hymn book which I had in my hand was very wet and almost un-readable. I learned to dance when I was sixteen years old and, because I was nervous my hands sweated even more. I had suffered from sweaty hands my whole life and I cursed the fact that one must always shake hands to greet others. I have asked dozens of doctors here in Finland and in Sweden about what causes sweaty hands but have not received any satisfactory response. Some doctors said it was due to weakness, but I knew it was not.

Then I discovered the main food substance that leads to allergies, I solved the riddle of food allergies and noticed that my sweaty hands had disappeared. The years passed. I played football and we advanced to Division 2. The training became more intense. I had nothing that could indicate a disease. As a twenty-year-old, I did army service, and it was also hard training. Pea soup with pork, the most common food in the arm, was not a problem for me. If I were to eat peas with pork today, I'd be in big trouble! This proves that at twenty-two years of age, the allergens found in pork and peas did not affect me. In my case, it was only between the ages of twenty-five and thirty that my severe allergies started. When I was in a grocery store and I heard a thirteen-year-old girl say to her mother, "I can't eat that." I asked myself, could the girl have food allergies at such a young age? The mother replied that she did. I asked if she had a pen and wrote on a piece of paper the foods that she may be allergic to. The mother asked me whether I was sure, and I said: Look at me, do I look sick?

If I ate everything then I would look terrible. The mother then looked at me as if I was a liberator. This proves that food allergies can arise in one's teens. In Finland and Sweden, about five percent of people suffer from food allergies, amounting to 800,000 people.

The summer of 1959 was hot, and I went to Gainsborough in England to study packing machines, in particular a new fast wrapping machine. I did not have to work but I thought that as I had the time, I should start putting together machines. When I got home, I went to see a Swiss man who was head of packing at a large candy factory in Stockholm. I knew the Swiss man beforehand in Helsinki. He honored me by coming out onto the stairs when I arrived, and I realized only later why he was so humble. When I was five yards from him, he said, "Now I think God must have sent you here. It is impossible to get hold of a packing machine repairman in Sweden today. You must come and help me," he said. I tried not to seem interested, even though the offer was good.

Stockholm

Then he raised the salary a little and before he started crying, I said: "Send the offer to me in Helsinki, I may accept it." As I was going, he shouted, I trust you!

Stockholm was a pleasant place in the 1960s. In 1963 I started studying engineering in the evenings. I was working very, hard eight hours in the daytime and then four hours at school in the evening. After five years of this, I realized that it was too much. I understood, why they say a manager does not last for more than five years. When I was about twenty-five years old, I got eczema on my face and hair bottom for the first time. You could say that my symptoms began when I was twenty-five years old.

If you are sporting when you are young, you often continue sporting when you are older. I was thirty years old almost-an-engineer. I begin raising my fitness level. I went to the police riding ground, which was close. After running 200 yards, I felt something weird in my throat and started coughing.

Then I came to a sharp curve and because it was dark, I did not see that there were two policemen approaching, riding. I ran into one of the horses.

The horse was not afraid, but I had a huge coughing fit. One of the policemen got down from his horse and asked if I needed an ambulance. I asked the police to wait and after a few minutes the coughing fit passed. The next day, I went to the factory doctor, who examined me carefully but found nothing. It was my throat that was swollen and when I raised my pulse it became even more swollen.

I had smoked cigarettes and cigars six months prior to this event and so I blamed everything on tobacco.

In 1969, I moved to Karlstad, Sweden where we would start building the world's largest paper machine. It was said from the beginning that there may not be a delay.

The whole machine was time-scheduled and aimed at minimizing delays. The machine went to America's Mid-South. I had to draw to the point that my eyes were bleeding.

Back in Helsinki

It was 1971 and I bought Helsingin Sanomat, a daily newspaper in Helsinki. I saw that an employer was seeking an engineer for packaging machines. I called the employer and asked about the role. The director asked if I knew about Rose Brothers packing machines and I said that I knew them like the back of my hand. I said that I had even worked in the Gainsborough factory for a whole summer. The director asked me what I had in mind for a monthly salary, and I secured a very good salary. The director coughed and cleared his throat and it surprised me that he did not want to haggle.

It was Friday when I arrived in Helsinki and I went to meet my new employer. I shoved him my grades and he began to look at them immediately. After a while, he said in a humorous way, "You've worked with packing machines for eight years?" I said, "Mostly with Rose machines."

"Think you can get an ice cream packing machine to work on Monday?"

"I think so," I replied.

He said that he had sold a machine to an ice-cream factory and following an accident it was now not working well. It was July, the high season for ice cream.

The machine should have been running twenty-four hours a day. Occasionally, the production manager would call and was so angry with the director that he thought he would come along the phone lines and strangle him.

Now I understood why he had not bargained when I asked for quite a high salary. I said that I would go there in the morning at seven and fix the machine. He promised to pay 600 Fmk, so I was well paid. I arrived at the factory and found parts for the machine. The machine worked perfectly, after five hours of work.

On Monday morning, I went to the ice-cream factory, and there stood my employer and the tough production manager, who were now best of friends. It was a true success story in which all were winners and my work at the firm began, in the best possible way.

My allergy problems had increased. I had more dermatitis on my scalp and even more eczema on my face, which came and went. During the summer, I had water blisters on the hands, but it troubled me not so much because they disappeared in September when it became a little colder.

Finland's economy began to rise during 1970s when a large war debt to Russia was paid in full.

The problem remained that there was too little capital, for small investors. Prosperity came to Finland slowly but did eventually come due to the fact that the Finnish people have always been hard workers.

It was 1977 when we went to the cottage, so my wife wondered why I had eczema on my face. I said that it always happened in the spring and it was now mid-May. I began to think that I had a pollen allergy. At times, I had the sniffles for a couple of days, and I knew it was not the usual sniffles.

I looked sinister due to the long pollen catkins, which this spring were long and had a lot of pollen.

However, I had two days of a runny nose when there was no pollen, which quashed the pollen theory. Now I also started suspecting mold spores as allergens. I went to doctor's library and borrowed all the books I could about mold spores. I found that the science of mold spores was vast. Now I had to choose between pollen and mold allergies. When it was winter, I could see whether mold bothered me, however the winter was rainy and did not have long cold spells. I kept up my search for pollen and mold. It would have been more serious if I had to choose between cancers and leprosy, don't laugh!

In the 1980s, I carried on and designed machinery for many industries, both large and small.

I then launched production and received a commission from Aylesbury Automation, who manufactured vibration machines. I was now fifty years old and had worked very hard. I had only two workers in the workshop and they were very highly skilled professionals.

Most days I worked from seven in the morning to seven in the evening.

My throat was sometimes so swollen that I could not sleep, and it was difficult to drive a long distance. Driving a car is dangerous if you are tired.

I worked like that for around five years until the banking crisis came. I was fifty-six years old when I began in earnest to find out what it was in my throat.

I had already started to lean towards the opinion that it was food allergy. I went to a clinic and there was an older doctor who examined me and said: "Asthma, you do not have but it is there in the throat. We must treat it." He sent me to a hospital where they filmed my throat. When the results from the hospital came, they did not show anything. I was filmed at 9 o'clock in the morning and had not eaten anything that swelled my throat. Two weeks later, my throat was so swollen that I could not sleep for two nights and I went to the clinic again. There was now a young doctor, who seemed fine, but he immediately began to believe it was asthma. I said what the older doctor had said that I did not have asthma.

He gave me four antihistamine tablets. When I took the antihistamines, they were not helpful, and today, with hindsight, I know why they did not help.

Antihistamines are supposed to neutralize amines but when there are so many different amines in the blood, one tablet does not help.

When I was fifty-nine, I started going to the gym so that I could "stop the aging process." At age of sixty-two, I could bench press 332 lb. lying on one's back and lifting a barbell straight up. Someone else lifted 10 lb. more than me. I did not understand why 332 lb. was my absolute limit. As a young man, I never lost out in strength to anyone.

When I lifted 8 x 222 lb., I started coughing. I knew there was something that took away my strength.

One morning when I was going to the gym, I had a steep hill to go up. It was minus five-degree Fahrenheit and whilst climbing up to the crest, I got a coughing attack and spat blood. It was awful, but I went to the gym anyway. I went to the doctor and told him that I had spat blood.

I noticed that the doctor was a little nervous and he told me I must go to the hospital for further tests. He wrote me a referral and I was on my way.

When I arrived at the hospital, I was told it was asthma, which they would seek. I was asked to give saliva and then given a tube to breathe into, the results of which were recorded.

Each day, I would blow into it without Ventolin (which opens the airways) and then I would blow into it again after taking Ventolin. I blew into the tube and it showed the maximum reading. I realized they had given me a short tube. I began to understand that this asthma test was completely unnecessary.

I took the test results to the hospital and the doctor looked at the bladder sample and gave me a longer blow tube. I could not help but be ironic, asking, "What's the world record?" The female doctor smiled just like the Mona Lisa.

When I received the long tube to blow into, I managed to blow it to the maximum again.

The following week they were filming my windpipe (Bronco Scopiad). There was a slight narrowing of one bronchus.

When I went to see the doctor, who had sent me for the asthma tests, he was almost sure it was asthma. He started talking about bronchi, but I interrupted him and told him, that the problem was in my throat, not bronchi. I also said that if at sixty-three years old, I had asthma then it would not be so difficult to observe. The doctor wrote out a prescription of Cortisone Discus which I was to inhale morning and evening.

I bought the Discus, but I refused to take the complete course that the doctor had prescribed.

After I took one inhalation I could sleep. I had a sister who was a head nurse at a large hospital in Miami, Florida, and she said that you only take cortisone when you know you will soon die.

In the United States, they had used cortisone a lot but now it was almost forbidden.

Cortisone hides cancers for a long time and gives sufferers less chance of survival.

One day whilst going to the city center by subway, I climbed a long flight of stairs and came out in the cold air of minus nine degrees, I coughed blood for the second time. I went to the doctor again. The doctor listened again to my bronchus and then wrote new referrals to the hospital.

When I got to the hospital, the doctor said that I would have a new asthma test. I said to the female doctor, "We will not have much fun," and I noticed that she was a little angry.

The female doctor had announced that I had no asthma, but the second doctor sent me for new asthma tests. We're getting nowhere with the testing for asthma, so I put a stop to it.

It was now the end of April. On evening, I noticed that I was starting to get blisters on my hands. It was one month too early. The blisters were so bad that the skin of my fingers came off.

I thought it must be food allergy and began to stop my intake of substances that are known to be allergens.

I also went to the doctor and showed him when the skin was gone. The doctor thought, that there was inflammation and told me to put ointment (Bactroban) on it.

I started to lose skin every week. The doctor wrote a prescription of ten penicillin tablets. At first, I decided not to take the tablets, but I had no choice. After taking the tablets only, the outer skin of the fingers came off, a thin layer. When the tablets had finished, the skin continued to peel as usual. I had heard that the hospital tests for allergy skin tests using allergens and tape on the back and arms. I went to the doctor to get a referral for such a test.

I went to the hospital and blood samples were first taken. I found out I had ESR above 20 mm. It is abnormal if depression is over 15 mm and I had 20 mm.

The doctor at the allergy hospital looked at my fingers, which were slightly swollen and full of water blisters. He did not know what it could be. He watched my fingers with a magnifying glass and shook his head.

Tape with allergens on it, was then put on my hands. The next test was a month later because it was Christmas.

One morning, whilst drinking my morning coffee I decided to fry an egg. I suddenly remembered that egg was an allergen, so I put it back in the fridge.

There had been new blisters on my fingers but by the middle of the day the development of the blisters, I saw, had reduced. Clearly, it meant that not eating the egg had a positive effect. The skin came off as usual but not as much as before.

This was the first indication that I had food allergy. I called the doctor at the allergy hospital and told him about the egg, which I did not eat. The doctor said: "Don't worry, we'll find out what you have, in the second test." I had a Dutch-Swedish medical book at home and had read about how it works, doubted that they would find food allergy.

It was not just a case of finding my food allergy but finding which was making me sick. I began to try and find the next food substance, which was an allergen. I could no longer talk to the doctors because they knew nothing.

Pork

My mother always said, when asked to do something: "Who lifts the cat's tail other than the cat itself." Now, my mother's words came in handy when I had no one to ask.

I called the State Food Laboratory, and a female laboratory manager answered.

I asked her which substances keeps meat red and fresh and she replied, "Do not worry about these topics they have been tested many times. Search for allergens in proteins instead." This was quite helpful to me.

From my mother, I had also got an "idea generator." When I constructed machines, I had much help from the generator but was it retired as I was? I once sold an electro scale to a female agronomist.

She gave me lunch, though it should have been the other way around. When we ate pork, she explained how pork had changed after they started to feed pigs, real food. My idea generator said *pork*.

I wondered if the idea generator really was awake but decided to try pork in all cases. There is pork in many foods. Sausages, for example, are almost exclusively pork and flour. I bought sirloin steak and ate it with potatoes and cucumber salad. I saw that there were no other substances, known to be allergens.

I had new skin on my fingers, and when the fingers did not begin to itch at noon, I thought that pork may be the big gangster.

The next morning came and dinner time I had no blisters. Could I really find the gangster in my first test? My idea generator worked just as in my youthful days. The next day I made a big mistake.

When I entered the store, I saw minced beef and remembered that it was good with garlic and chili.

I bought five ounces, and of course, it was good when I fried it with plenty of garlic. The garlic should be roasted for only half a minute so that it remains semi-rough. The next day my fingers started to itch at 11:00 am and I wondered why.

The next day, I went to the store and asked the store manager whether it was possible that pork had been in the minced beef. "It is possible," said the manager, "a little pork could remain in the meat."

I told him why it was so important, and the store manager said that he will go and make minced beef again for me that would be guaranteed to be free of pork. He gave me the package and said it was free of charge.

After eating the minced beef, I was sure that the skin would not come off my fingers.

The next day came and the clock hit twelve, one and two. I was sure that pork was great *Al Capone*. I said to my idea generator, "Sorry! I'm getting old."

It was now time for the big prick tests that required fifty-five different allergens to be taped on my back. I knew how unnecessary it was to go there but had to do it anyway. I went for the test and after two week I went back to meet an allergy doctor.

The allergy doctor looked at the result and said: "You have no allergies, I guarantee it."

I knew from the start that this would happen, and I was indifferent to everything else as I had found that pork was the problem. By now I had experienced the skin coming off my fingers every week for eight months.

I noticed now that things had happened in my body and I was feeling much better. When I was at the gym, I noticed that my strength started to come back. I bench pressed 310 lb. and increased this to 322 lb., lifting it with speed.

I knew now that pork had not only removed the skin from my fingers, but also my strength. If this search for the allergen was like a tennis match, then I had won the first set.

I was interested to find out the results of the blood tests and I went to the laboratory.

In order to know the blood tests, I had to go to the doctor, who had thought I had asthma. The doctor was almost afraid to see me and said that I had a blood sedimentation rate of only 11; it had been 22 mm. He asked if there had been any change in my life and I said that I had removed pig meat from my diet.

The doctor said very slowly, "Pork!" I told the doctor that, "you learn, as long, as you live!"

At the gym, I set out to do hard training. I wanted to see what a sixty-five-year-old could lift in the bench press.

I had learned a new training method; only three times at maximum weight, then rest for one day. The following day do these three lifts again, then rest for two days.

Through this method one can lift 5 lb. more. Using this method, I proceeded until I had reached 355 lb. Then something happened, and I went back again. I was at the same level for two weeks and then started to move forward again. I came to 360 lb. and again could not lift more.

After a week on a Saturday, I felt that my strength had come back.

I told two of my friends that we should go to the gym and that they would see me lift 355 lb. Anyone who believes that it is only strength that is needed for the bench press is wrong.

If one does not put hands in the right place, one can never lift big weights. When I tried 355 lb., everything went 100% right. A physical education teacher said it was a beautiful lift and therefore proceeded easily.

I got eleven percent more strength when my blood sedimentation rate went from 22 to 11. Each time I was at the gym I could lift 355 lb.

A year passed, and it was spring. I thought about trying to lift over 355 lb. on bench press.

I started with 335 lb. and undertook two weeks of strength training, I again lifted 355 lb. and the way was paved for me to try 360 lb.

I was warming up, to get blood to my muscles when I noticed to my horror that 330 lb. already felt heavy. There was no point in trying more. There were still allergens, playing tricks on me, but it is only with hind-sight, that this can be said easy.

Doctors, researchers, and professors have searched for a hundred years without finding out that pork is a problem, even though I found out in two months.

Every morning a little brown substance would come from my throat, a lining, which was not good. Sometimes when sleeping I had a problem with my throat. Sometimes I would take antihistamine, but sometimes I would have to take cortisone. However, I did not give up hope of finding the allergen that was making my life difficult.

After going through these surveys, it surprised me a lot about how little doctors know about food allergy. It should be a scientist or doctor who has food allergies that seeks to identify allergies. A doctor who has food allergy would have been much more likely to find pork or vegetable oil as allergens. It was previously known that soy oil was an allergen, but why did they not find the other vegetable oils.

At the time of writing, I do not know what it is in oil that causes symptoms. I think it is the size of the fat acid. When I was searched for the allergens that were making me sick, there was a doctor who said that I should change my environment. This is what made me decide to move to Spain.

Espania Por Favor

I was lucky that it was Spain because they use olive oil in their foods, which was an important factor in my being able to explain; why vegetable oils contain allergens.

In 2004, I happened to be in the wrong place at the wrong time. It was April and I was perhaps tired of the quiet days in Helsinki.

I had no woman to keep an eye on. I was free to come and go in the sunshine and in the rain. I happened to meet someone who owned an apartment in Spain.

I said just in jest, are you allowed to rent to me? I could imagine that he did not have much time to travel to Spain. I told him about my allergy problems and the man said, "Go for a week at first, just to try it." I went to Alicante in early May.

The site was thirty miles from Alicante and belonged to the town of Orihuela, which was a fifteen-mile inland. The place was called Orihuela Costa.

No Margarin

The day before I went there, it was seventy-five degrees Fahrenheit in Helsinki. When I came to Alicante it was only sixty-six degrees Fahrenheit. The apartment where I lived where inhabited mostly by Germans and Spaniards, and there were five English families. For me it was not so important that it should be hot, I just wanted to see what it was like to live there. I began to investigate where I could get food because I could not eat eggs and pork.

There were three large supermarkets 200 yards away from where I lived so it was easy to get food.

The apartment where I lived was modern and everything was almost perfect. The weather was bad but that is the way it is sometimes.

Only after 15th May that you can be sure it will be hot. I went to the biggest supermarket and was a long time there. I saw what I needed for a week. I took a package of margarine in my hand but put it back.

I saw that there were small butter packages next to it. I did not need a pound of margarine for one week.

I took eight small packs of butter and this came to play an important role in my search for allergens. I bought one kilograms of cheap beef, which I then cooked. I bought five pieces of steak which I froze at home. I also bought large potatoes and vegetables.

I had bought the Spanish textbook, 'Este pais' in Helsinki and when it was raining; I thought I would read Spanish.

I lived on the edge of the old fishing town of Torrevieja, the center of which was six yards.

One could take a bus to Torrevieja town center and the bus was always crowded. So, went the week in Spain and when I got home at night it was being said over the airline speakers that it was minus twenty-six Fahrenheit in Helsinki. It was plus seventy-six when I left!

On the plane, I had ordered food for allergies and it was good because I felt nothing in the morning. When I was travelling to Spain, I had the same allergy food and I had suffered a little from bad throat the next morning. I now know why it was so.

When I came from Finland the food was cooked in rapeseed oil but when I returned from Spain it was olive oil.

I had now decided to move to Orihuela Costa because I felt good the week I was there. I now had two weeks to get rid of everything. When you have lived for twenty years in one place, you have a lot of unnecessary things. I was mad at myself that I had saved completely useless and unnecessary things. It was a sweaty job to get rid of everything in two weeks. I told my friends: "The grass is greener on the other side!" There I stood as a Buddhist monk waiting for my flight to Alicante.

When I arrived in Alicante, I was met with seventy-eight-degree Fahrenheit of heat. More people had arrived at the apartments.

After 15th May it was guaranteed to be warm in Torrevieja. It has the highest number of sunny days in a year in the whole of Europa. This was now my new life in Spain.

I had studied Spanish for a month and was not completely ignorant of Spanish. I also spoke English, German and Swedish so I had no problem *talking*.

There was now a lot of work to be done. First, I would put in the papers for residence, and it was hard work ensuring the papers were perfect. To submit the papers, it took three hours and if you had anything wrong in the papers or something was missing you had to come again the next day and queue for another three hours.

I enrolled myself at gym that was located 1 mile from my home. At the gym, there were mostly Englishmen, Germans, Norwegians, and Swedes. Everyone was about my age give or take around five years. There was a young Greek who was thirty years old. He was big and strong. He weighed 30 lb. more than me and I thought that he would beat me in the bench press.

The move to Spain had meant that I was only able to lift some 320 lb. in the bench press. But then it emerged that the great Greek could not lift more than 245 lb. I was champion again.

The bread in Spain was a problem as it got quickly moldy. I bought Swedish crisp bread and tasted half a piece immediately.

I also bought a wheat baguette, which was fresh and crispy. It was good bread. I bought this bread many times. I started getting eczema on my chest just as if I had eaten eggs. I had met a German woman and we would walk to Torrevieja together. I asked her if she would like to drink a cup of tea before going. I wondered why I got eczema on my chest. I had not eaten eggs in a year. When she took the bread, she said, "You have egg in this bread which is why it is crispy." There are traps everywhere for allergy sufferers.

I wondered what might be causing my constant weight loss. I thought that I should go to the doctor when I lost weight. The next day I was in Torrevieja and as it was thirty degrees, for once I decided to drink a beer.

At the other table sat a guy who said he was from London. He had been a great sportsman and we got talking. Before I left, I asked him what may be causing my weight loss.

He asked me how much I had gone down, and I said eights pounds in two weeks. "You have worms!" he said. "Have a great cure for those that are hard to get rid of." I had to take two courses as the first did not help. The London guy was right they can be difficult to get rid of.

As I went home from the gym, I came to a small restaurant where I saw two ladies, who also went to the gym. One was English and the other Norwegian. The English lady said, "Sit down awhile and rest."

I sat down and talked about my worms. When I mentioned worms, the Norwegian lady began to laugh, almost unhindered, because we shopped in the same supermarket. The Norwegian lady then said, "Have you bought milk crisp?" I said that I had and that there were so many worms in the package that it almost walked by itself. As crisp bread is hard, the Spaniards believe that it keeps forever. "Crisp bread is forever," just like diamonds. July and August are a little too hot for northerners. I once went

back and forth to Torrevieja in eighty-eight-degree
Fahrenheit heat I drank nothing on the road.

Heavenly Beautiful

It is a distance of seven mile. Today's youth must have a drink with them if they go more than one mile. When it was very hot, I went down to the beach and swam a while.

I would lie there on my back without sinking, as the water was so salty that you would float.

At home, I had a table wheremy Spanish textbook was always open. If you turn off and put away a book it will be a long time before you read it again. This is an important point to remember if you want to read intensely.

After four months, I had grasped the basics. I now speak four languages quite well and Spanish pretty well.

If I were able to determine the main language for Europe, it would be Spanish.

Once when I was walking in Torrevieja, I saw a man, middle aged, who was singing but he was not drunk. I recognized the melody and asked, "What's the song?" He looked at me very surprised and said, "Sielito lindo," and I understood immediately that it meant Heavenly Beautiful. The Spaniard felt that I was unique in that, I wanted to talk to him. He asked where I came from and thought that I must have been living here a longtime. I said that I had only lived here seven months but that it was easy to learn Spanish from Swedish.

I then looked on Google and learned the words to "Sielito lindo" and now I sing it as well. I dare not sing it in Helsinki on the street because maybe they would come and take me away. The words are: *Ow, ow, ow, ow sing and weep not, for when you sing it is so heavenly beautiful in our hearts.*

My health was not as good as it was the week after I had arrived. I had a little tickle in my throat, and it was a little brown in color, indicating that the lining of the throat was inflamed.

You could say that I felt the same as when I had arrived. The winter passed and spring came.

One day in early June, my German friend came and told me with tears in her eyes that her mother had died.

She had already started planning the trip home. She returned to Germany on June 15. When I went to swim in the pool there was an old German there. He was there for a few weeks as someone's guest, who I knew. The man said he had been a prisoner of war in Siberia for eighteen years. He knew not what kept the spark of life within him for eighteen years in that hell and said: "I have been a free man since the mid-1960s, but I still wake up every morning there."

As I could speak Spanish it was interesting living in Spain but the poor infrastructure and the fact that the German women who was a good company went home, when her mother died; I began to look towards the north. In August I went to Helsinki and prepared for my comeback. I went to the gym and an Englishman asked, "Where were you last week?" I said I was in Hell…sinki. The big Englishman said to the others, "He was in hell for a week."

After two weeks, I was ready to go home. On my last day at the gym, I told the two Englishmen, who used to joke with me, that I was moving home.

Home Sweet Home

One of them asked, "You are going home to the cold Finland?"

"Yes," I said and started singing "Green Grass." The other one shouted, "He is travelling to Finland to be hanged." There was a huge roar of laughter in the whole gym. On my journey I had too much weight in my luggage. You could have 56 lb. altogether and I had 20 lb. too much. I said in flawless Spanish: I am moving home now and have a little too heavy luggage. The Spaniard, who was in control, said "Vale", is equivalent of "OK." I had the economic advantage of my language skills.

In October, I was back in Helsinki and had time to prepare for winter. I was thinking about not getting a car. I did not need a car in Helsinki because the traffic is so developed. I was going everywhere by bus, train, and metro. At my age, I must walk 5000 steps per day if I want to keep the cartilage in my knees.

A couple moved in next door; they had a Mercedes Benz.

I noticed that the man was a little cautious when he stepped out of his Mercedes. A year later he sold his Mercedes and bought himself a walker. He tried for a year to go around with the walker but then gave up. Today he is in a wheelchair, due to the fact, that the cartilage in his knees is completely gone.

Doctors warn you, that you must start walking, in time. Mercedes Benz should produce walking frames so that one who drives his car for a long time can get the same logo on his walker.

Life was good in Helsinki because I had a perfect location for access to the places I wanted to go.

When walking to the gym and to the city center, I would walk more than twelve mile a week. I needed fifteen miles. I got exercise for free.

The man of today does not really know what he needs to do at the moment. We should constantly ask ourselves "is it right," as I now do. The brain must keep up with every move we make.

Lidl opened a store in the city. They sold deep frozen sirloin steak which came from Argentina.

At first, I was afraid of the steak, as it had a marinade on it. When I saw that it was harmless, I ate it for the first time in two and a half years. I did not notice that the importing country had changed. I started to get eczema and my throat became a little more swollen. One time I happened to look at the package and noticed that the steak came now from New Zealand. I ended up buying that steak and the eczema disappeared.

One day I looked at the steak package with a magnifying glass and saw that it had "corn" bonded brackets. I understood that they meant there was corn oil present in it.

Before I had put away eggs and pork, and now I also tried to put away margarine and rapeseed oil.

I remember the time just after the war when margarine came to the market. It was yellow and did not taste so good. My mother made butter if she could get the milk. When we had butter, it was like Christmas Eve. I used only butter for a week, but it had no positive effect, so I started using margarine again as it was so healthier.

One day I got a lot of eczema and my throat was worse as well. I wondered whether I could ever have a better health. I then used my "idea generator." It had collected data from all the unusual names and it now said: "Try margarine again!" I remember that during the week in Spain I never bought margarine. That week was now the most important evidence that margarine should be put to "death." I was sure about olive oil, so I bought a big bottle I also bought butter. In the afternoon, it struck me that either margarine or oil in bread. I remembered that I was an excellent baker. I began to bake buns with butter. The buns were very good and warm, and I ate them with butter and evening tea. When I went to sleep, I had a swollen throat, so I took an antihistamine. I lay there and wondered why things were so. Was there anything strange about the flour?

I got up and looked at the flour bag and it said that there were 0.07 ounce of fat in 3.5 ounce of flour. I lay on the bed and went through the day's events again.

Now I was almost sure that it was all vegetable oils, which were allergens.

The Fabulous Evening

I would have to wait until tomorrow.

In the morning, I had three boiled potatoes and boiled beef. I was drinking morning tea with my potatoes, beef, and vegetables. I ate nothing that could have jeopardized this great moment because I knew that I had won the second set in a three sets match and thus the whole match. <u>Vegetable oil</u> was for me, Al Capone's brother.

The very next day in the evening, I found that my nose was completely open, as well as my throat. Now I could sing Sielito lindo (Heavenly Beautiful).

It was a training day at the gym, and I knew that my strength had returned. I had lost weight 13 lbs. and could only lift 288 lbs. in the bench press, which was my absolute maximum. I went from 265 lbs. to 290 and it went up with ease. I lifted the same weight three times and promised the guys at the gym that in about two days I would lift 300 lbs., which I did. In one and a half weeks I was up 310. At sixty-six years of age, I could lift 355 lb.

If I had known that vegetable oil was an allergen, I would have lifted 375 lb. I told the guys at the gym that I now lived in a state of NIRVANA.

When going to buy food, I knew in advance that it was difficult to find food as one can assume that pig meat, eggs, fish, and vegetable oil is present in 80% of our food. I have talked to those who have food allergies and they all say, "I am allergic to all foods." It is difficult to find any food, which does not contain the above substances. The young may not be allergic to them yet, but it is good to keep these substances in your mind because you might become allergic to them later in life.

I am 74 years old today and you can be sure that I have the worst allergies, but today I suffer from almost no symptoms and I have lived like this for five years. In these five years, I have had to avoid vegetable oil which is almost in everything.

Now that you have read about my struggle with food allergy which four or five doctors were helpless to find, you may ask how the female health minister could say that, "Food allergies are very well known."

I wrote my book in Swedish and a book publisher printed the book and began selling it online. A week later, when I realized how difficult it was to get food, I sent an e-mail to the Swedish Minister of Health. I told her how hard it was to get food.

The Swedish Minister of Health is also a woman and is a friend of the Finnish minister.

The two ministers are also in the same political party, which is right wing.

When reading the book that I sent her the Swedish minister would see that the reason I wrote the book in Swedish was that I was turned down for help by the Finnish minister. (They possibly had contact with each other). After half a year, the Swedish minister said that she did not have time. In my mail, I said that there were 450,000 food allergy sufferers in Sweden and that many may be in pain. My whole life I have wondered why most people never grow up. It is the narcissist that control.

In most countries political direction is the most important.

The European Union now also works in political groups. If you have the same political ideas, you are considered OK. I have noticed that teachers, psychologists, and doctors are not that interested in politics. It is of course linked to their profession, but I thought they are a little more mature people.

I went to Stockholm and attempted to get Academy Bookstore to sell my book as they have so many stores nowadays. The female managers read the book and then said that she did not want to take it up for sale. The book was then presented at the book fair in Gothenburg, Sweden.

I had fifteen minutes to talk about the book. When I came to the sentence, "I have solved food allergies" there was one person drinking coffee whose coffee nearly went down the wrong way. An old lady came up to me and said, "You have bitten off more than you can chew." The lady was apparently a retired doctor.

Albert Einstein did not attend the University of Zurich, but the headmaster offered him the position of janitor there.

Albert Einstein

The rector said although everyone may not be geniuses, all must eat. Although Albert was a caretaker, he did not feel inferior. He talked to the professors, even though he had a janitor's hat on his head.

Albert felt that the professors were friendly as they smiled at him and he presumed that they understood everything he was saying as they did not ask anything. There was talk and jokes about Albert's ideas and Albert had become a world fool. There had never been so much fun at the Zurich University before. A professor at Oxford got the second letter. He was serious even after the first letter as, it matched a little with his own wild thoughts. After getting the second letter, he grabbed his pen and wrote to Zurich: "Your caretaker Albert Einstein is correct, in everything he says."

The letter had the effect of a letter bomb. All looked at each other with a sinister stare. There had never been such an uncomfortable mood at Zurich University.

It took me six years to find the allergen that was making me sick and that is a short time, if you think, that doctors and professors have not find all allergens in a hundred years. It is peculiar that they do not understand a ready solution to food allergy problem. The Swedish book has been on sales for one year and seven months and I know that doctors have read the book. Probably even a professor has read the book. In the Swedish book, I wrote that I had not received any help from a doctor other than the disservice when they diagnosed me as having no allergies, which they were sure of. My youngest sister was a teacher in Malmö, Sweden, and she had such a swollen throat that it was difficult for her to stand in front of a class. A professor in Malmö, Sweden was trying to find out what was wrong with her but found nothing.

I would occasionally buy beef and find that there was nothing on the package stating that there was vegetable oil in it.

I made contact with the Food Safety Authority and told them that it should not be vegetable oil in beef because that is my only source of protein. They said nothing.

Then I found out that they could do nothing without the Agriculture and Forestry Minister's permission. The Agriculture and Forestry Minister's was a woman, so I was almost sure I would not get a response. I sent an email to her anyway, in which I stated that it was very difficult to get pure beef and that there were 275,000 food allergy sufferers in Finland. I asked in big letters whether she wanted to help all those with allergies. She did not reply.

Finland and Sweden are trying to get a 50/50 split of men and women in government and in large government agencies as part of their affirmative action policies otherwise it is not democracy. The one who understands psychology well knows that it is the same as making the national football team half men and half women. This year, two female ministers had to stop because of incompetence.

A girl plays with dolls until she is seven or eight years of age, she then begins to make herself pretty and attractive and all other things that are hormone-driven.

When she becomes a woman and is intelligent, and gets academic training and then, a high level of employment, she has achieved something that she did not get from her childhood.

A human being is born with an almost perfect brain, but there is nothing in one's memory to compare things with.

When I was about three years old, a Russian bomb fell only 100 yards from my two sisters and me. The pressure of the bomb pushed me into a deep ditch. I heard the blast but did not know what it was. I did not think it was Stalin, who wanted to kill me. The only thing that I had in my small memory was that my sister sometimes joked with me and, so it was she who had pushed me into the ditch. When I, with great effort, came up from the ditch, I was very angry at my sister, "for playing such a childish joke."

A man (takes his "operating systems") develops his intellect from birth to six years and he follows it throughout his live. It is the quality of this intellect that determines what he will become. For a large international company, it is vital that they get a capable president. In politics, you can enter through the "back door" and become a minister.

You need not be a "gunpowder inventor" but you must be able to take people in the right way. It is an advantage if you are a great sportsman or beauty queen. I, as a trained engineer have looked many times in horror what has become of government ministers in Finland.

It has been five years since I found all the allergens that were affecting me and now live a healthy life. The biggest problem has been getting pure meat.

I wrote this book in Finnish, and took contact with the Prime Minister, who is also a woman. The Prime Minister promised to read the book, which I sent to her as a PDF file. Nothing happened!

I also sent the book to the former president, who is a woman, but she did not want to read the book. She is a social democrat.

When the new male president was installed, I got an e-mail that he wanted to read my book. The new president is from Coalition Party (right-wing).

The new prime minister is also from the same party as the health minister, who initially said: "Food-allergy is well known," and did not respond to my new email, she is from the same party.

I asked for help from three Ministers + Prime Minister + President, all from the Coalition Party, if they want to help me plus the 270,000 food allergy sufferers to get foodso that we can live a healthy life.

I thought, *is it like this that the Soviet Union scientists felt under Stalin's regime*. My fears came true because I got absolutely no response from the President.

A new President usually always certified that he/she is everyone's president. It is possible that our current president also affirmed that he is everyone's president, but it was certainly not so for many who believed him.

I then sent the book to the Chancellor of Justice and asked if a minister can determine that my book is not worth exploring.

Now that this book has been published in English, it may be read by a professor, who can write to our Prime Minister, and state that: Everything, which the author says is true because you become healthy and you can test this with the "Super Diet" in this book.

Now you need help getting food.

Super Diet

I made this diet to give food allergy sufferers a rock whereby he/she can feel safe:

Meat: In this SUPER DIET it should be the meat of a BULL because it may be whey or a hormone found in cow meat. A CALF has no whey in the blood till about one year. You can eat the veal if it is controlled, the meat of the bull must be prepared in excess of 212-degree Fahrenheit heat. Smoked meat or semi-raw steak can produce eczema.

With MUTTON, the same applies to cattle. FISH (fish that eat fish and only MALE FISH). People with food allergies can eat only male animal. OLIVE OIL (Fat from the trees is OK). POTATO (boiled potatoes are recommended).

ONIONS (all onions, garlic lowers the blood pressure). CABBAGE HEAD, CHINESE-CABBAGE (not cabbage with flowers). CUCUMBER, LETTUCE BLACKCURRANT JUICE (contains fiber, which is needed,

TEA, (normal tea)

APPLES (Pare the apples if they are both) CALCIUM TABLETS (with vitamin D).

(Talk to a doctor about calcium and see to ensure there is no vegetable oil in the tablets).

Remember! No vegetable fat and no whey.

The meat of the bull must be prepared in excess of 212 degrees F. Smoked meat or semi-raw steak can produce eczema.

As you can see, milk products are completely left out of the list of food stuff in the diet. There is a large number that are good to have in one's diet. I have been unable to test milk products because I am apparently intolerant to lactose. Milk fat should not be an allergen because it is cattle produce milk. I will leave dairy products, for someone else to research.

When trying to find new food substances, I would group them into families.

When after six years, I found that margarine/rapeseed oil and fat were present in bread it was clear that all vegetable oils were allergens.

To the scientists, I would say that various vegetable oils can cause eczema in different part of the body. All grains contain vegetable oils and should not be eaten by food allergic which removes a large group of food substances from their diet. I am beginning more and more leaning towards the theory that it is for the most part the major fatty acids and whey which cause food allergy. The major fatty acid molecules are also in plants as in animals.

I can eat elk steak but not reindeer steak; it depends on what they eat. Give no vegetable fat to cattle before slaughter.

If we go back to the SUPER DIET, we can see the main protein source is bull meat.

They put vegetable oil in almost all bull meat sauce, so you understand how difficult it is to live in Finland and Sweden, if you are allergic to certain foods.

When I first entered a shop after finding out that vegetable oil was an allergen, I realized that potatoes were my salvation.

Leningrad Rescue

Potatoes also once came to Leningrad's rescue. In fact, potatoes are just as sacred in Leningrad as the cow is in India. The best vegetable source of amino acids is potato. Potatoes also contain sugar and vitamin C. When I see someone who cannot manage to eat all their food, it is always the potatoes they leave. However, they are in fact leaving the best part.

In the West, we eat an excessive amount of protein. These days I do not eat much protein, and I am surely one of Europe's strongest 72-year-old (322 lbs.).

When you drink juice, which should not contain histamine, it may be that you get a slightly runny nose.

Juice manufacturer do not clean the containers, so there remains a little juice, which contain histamine and that gives you the sniffles. Fruits and berries that causes symptoms are: avocado, citrus fruits, raspberries, and strawberries.

Vegetables that cause symptoms: beans, spinach, tomatoes, nuts, and there is vegetable oil!

There are certainly more fruits and berries, which produce symptoms, and there are many who give no symptoms so, I will not list them here. The substances that cause the most serious problems are pork, (vegetable oil is in pork) vegetable oil, eggs, birds. Now I have listed these it will leave much in the shop that you can eat.

You need to get the twenty amino acids for cell building and you get these from meat. However, it is not healthy to only eat meat. Earlier I mentioned that potatoes were an excellent source of amino acids.

The organism synthetizes amino acids of that which is most easy, and the potatoes are very appropriate.

Of the twenty amino acids, there are eight which the organism cannot synthesize, so, meat, eggs, fish, and more are needed.

If you have food allergies you should keep them holy: the potato, like Leningrad residents and the bull, like Indians.

Food allergy eczema is always of the same nature. There is a swelling under your skin is fluid (sweat).

Now that you have the SUPER DIET available you can stop your intake of the allergens that cause the swelling. However, you must puncture the skin, to get the fluid out. You burn a needle and then make around four to five holes in your skin to try to get the fluid out. If you do not take the fluid out, it will take a long time to get rid of the eczema. You can talk to a doctor about this.

Histamine swells the fine blood vessels so that blood comes through. Histamine is contained in a blood cell called basophils granulocytes. When it comes out and free in the blood, it swells a little here and there. When an amine swells, the sweat glades open. A hormone should do this when you are hot. A doctor can explain this to you.

You will notice how much benefit you get from the SUPER DIET as you will learn what produces symptoms such as eczema.

When examining any topic, take one subject at a time and try it for three days. If it does not cause symptoms, it is OK.

I think that researchers will also produce a good SUPER DIET as they continue to search for substances in food and cause reactions in the human body.

Six years ago, I was a sick man, and then I went through the processes which I have described in this book. It has always surprised me how little doctors and professors know about food allergies. After all, they are linked to the food we eat every day.

I am glad that I got into this quest. The worst part was when I lost the skin off my two fingers every week and my throat was so swollen that I could not swallow and could not sleep. Four years ago, when I found that all vegetable oils were a problem, it was a relief that is hard to describe. All that I had complained to doctors about was gone. No, penicillin and cortisone were needed, and I am so fortunate now that I need absolutely no medicine.

I have not mentioned anything about the impact of alcohol on food allergies and I do not know much about the issue.

I stopped using alcohol completely when I was sixty.

I met a man early in the morning. He was very concerned because he could not sleep. When I asked, what was bothering him it became clear to me that the man had a food allergy. He had drunk quite a lot of beer the previous evening and he had a slight hangover.

When I told him what he could eat he became almost angry and said: I have talked to ten doctors about this, but they offered me no help. I also told him that he should not drink beer if he has food allergies, but then he did not continue the conversation.

Alcohol is in fact a narcotic and it seems to help when one is intoxicated, however researchers will tell you how alcohol affects food allergies.

Alcohol is the major scourge of the West and Russia as well as other places. Alcoholism is an incurable disease and a food allergy too.

But if you have a food allergy, you can now live happily with this book's help. I have had a good life and reached old age and when I die it will be without remorse knowing that I had not lived in vain.

WARNING! When this book comes out the food industry will not be aware that vegetable oil is a strong allergen.

Vegetable oil, especially corn oil and soy oil are the biggest problem because they put it on all beef meat. I think that pork meat is the same as soy because they feed the pigs with soy. I think that all vegetable oil is the main cause to food allergy problems.

An animal that eats foodstuffs containing vegetable oils will end up with them in their bloodstream. The cattle cannot eat vegetable fats just before slaughter.

In the countries where this book comes out, the responsible minister should ensure that there is to learn which foods that can be eaten; those not containing vegetable fats. You have read in the book how I found the various vegetable oils, one at a time, and then I was completely without food allergy symptoms.

Explanation of Vegetable Fat

My sedimentation rate decreased from 22 mm to 5 mm. My general condition went from very sick to perfect health. There must be vegetable oil, which is the general cause of food allergies.

Various vegetable oils give eczema, at different places on the body. You get sicker if you eat multiple vegetable fats than if you eat only one.

In pork, there are soy and fat from corn and therefore, it is a very strong allergen. My sedimentation rate went from 22 to 11 mm when I stopped eating pork.

There are amines, which swells here and there and opens e.g., sweat glands. When I ate soy and some other fat, I lost skin from two fingers, when I ate bread and margarine fat, I got swollen throat. When I ate corn fat and rapeseed oil, I got big dermatitis of the neck. When I ate eggs, I got eczema on my chest.

I do not know how this is true for other people, but I have an indication that it is the same body part the eczema comes, but not exactly, the same spot.

The different fats swell in some different place and of course several if you eat different fats, you get more swellings.

I helped one that had white gloves on both hands. The skin came off near the wrist. I asked him to stop eating especially pork and his eczema disappeared in three days.

In Finland, the doctors have given penicillin when the skin comes off, but I ask them only to stop eating pork. When I lived in Spain, I knew I must not eat pork, but I ate bread and margarine and then I had throat swollen but in the Spanish beef, there was no vegetable oil.

If the Spaniards must put oil together with nitrite on the beef it is olive oil.

It is popular to go to the Far East, but a person with food allergy should not go there because there is vegetable oil in everything.

In Spain, you must buy bull fillets from Spanish commercial stores, for corn oil has also come there. In restaurants, it is corn oil on bull fillets.

I sometimes got eczema and swollen throat after I ate sirloin steak.

I immediately sent an email to the Minister and the store that sold the meat, and they answered: We put nothing in the flesh guaranteed.

The female director of the Food Safety Authority read the book three and a half years ago, and she knew that it could be vegetable fat in the blood.

She is a doctor and she would have saved many from eczema if she had forbidden them to give rapeseed oil to the cow just before slaughter. This was a malicious act against me and 275,000 others with food allergies when she did not do anything.

I have talked only about beef meat and you might think it is the worst containing vegetable oil.

Bull meat is the only meat that I can eat if they do what I have told. I cannot go to Sweden, Germany, England, because I cannot get meat that keeps me healthy.

It is a big problem that people find difficult to understand. In Finland, we have five percent of those with food allergies and it makes 275,000 people.

In Sweden, it is 500,000. In Germany, there are about four to five million with food allergies.

I wonder what all allergic people will think when they read how doctors, professors, ministers and presidents of Finland and Sweden have refused me any help to provide them a healthy life.

I have written this book, almost like my memoir and then it is many, who recognize the symptoms they have had.

The problem in Finland and Sweden has been: No one believes in what I write because I cannot put the professor's title before my name and professors cannot help those with food allergies.

When I was into machine manufacturing, I did some machines, such as those in England, Germany and France was unable to do.

It is the one who has the ideas, who can do more difficult things regardless what he has for a title.

If you have read this book and then try to buy food so you probably wonder how you can live with so little food.

I have lived in six years with a simple diet without getting help from anyone. Mind you! Not a single person from doctors to presidents and it takes three days to test whether I am right or wrong.

I survived the war when I could not eat every day so I cannot imagine how difficult for young people this food issue is.

There has never been any medicine for food allergy, and it is unlikely that it will come, in the near future. The only help for those with food allergies is: THIS BOOK and your COMMON SENSE.

Continue!

Post Scriptum

Our biggest ski king died at 77. He was a reindeer herder from Pello in Lapland, Finland. The year before he died, he was on TV. I was appalled when I saw his face; it was full of eczema.

I knew immediately that he had food allergy and ate reindeer meat.

I found his phone number and called Pello. His wife answered and could not believe that the eczema came from reindeer meat.

Eero Mäntyranta was his name and he had many Olympic gold medals and was a considerate and reticent man. He had hemoglobin at approximately 200 and it may be the one that took his life at age 77, but he would have survived the last six years a better life if the doctor would have been able to understand my food allergy book.

Party leaders in Finland should have better knowledge of psychology when choosing a minister specifically the Minister of base service. These four female ministers have now delayed aid to allergic people in 10 years.

In the world, there are 550 million food allergy sufferers.

This English version, of my food allergy book, was already written seven years, ago.

I have sent it to Oxford University, but I do not know why they do not answer me? I have also tried to get it to Europe, but it also seems to be impossible.

Now we got a new government in Finland and I had a familiar minister there, who contacted the Minister of Basic Services. A person with food allergy can now eat bull meat without getting symptoms. It was the first time in six years I received help with getting food I can eat. A person with food allergy can now eat beef without getting symptoms.

I ate butter and had noticed that it was brighter than before. It must be because butter contains whey.

I bought a beater and made butter. I failed, and I got very bright butter. When I ate the butter, I got something in the large intestine.

It was as if it would have been wound or eczema. I noticed that I need a stronger beater. I now had a beater of 900 W and see!

I now got really, yellow butter, and when I ate the butter, the eczema of the scalp began to reduce and the wound in the intestine decreased.

It was ten years ago when I met a childhood friend, who was then 66 years old. He told me that he had wounds on large intestine. They had cut the large intestine and put it to rest. He had a bag on his stomach. After some weeks, they sewed the thick gut again and I thought it was good. I moved to Spain and met my old childhood friend. After one and a half years, I came back from Spain and was told that my childhood friend had died of cancer.

I wrote earlier in the book that I cannot say anything about dairy products because I cannot consume them.

However, I have eaten butter, but now I think I cannot eat dairy products at all.

I have asked the minister to request butter manufacturers if they can make butter where there is no whey. It is perhaps best for a food allergy sufferer to leave out all dairy products.

The milk protein is WHEY. I found out that whey was a nasty allergen.

It was also the first that gave me eczema of the scalp, and now, when I am old, it makes the wounds of the colon. When I looked into the new government, I saw to my delight that it was a male health minister. After my request, he ordained that the bull may not eat vegetable fat before slaughter. It worked well for a month.

When I bought sirloin for the fourth time, I had eczema of the scalp. It was immediately clear to me that there is whey. A cow has whey in the blood. This will cause a new problem for food allergy sufferers because it is expensive to eat sirloin every day. Sheep meat may be available and it is good in the summers when they do not get corn or rapeseed but you can eat only the male sheep. Laboratory engineers must begin researching how food allergy sufferer's protein needs can be satisfied.

The different allergens give symptoms in different places on and in the body. If we start with the allergen whey, which is a difficult allergen, because it attacks sensitive places, such as the nose, throat and the colon.

There is some swelling and then the skin is destroyed. If you stop eating whey, then it only takes six weeks until the eczema is gone. It is possible that it causes cancer.

The other troublesome allergen is the vegetable fat, which should be the same in all substances, but it does cause symptoms in different places on and in the body. If I eat eggs where there is vegetable fat from cereals, and I get eczema on the chest and something on the face. If I eat rapeseed oil (margarine) I get the eczema on the neck mostly.

The eczema from the vegetable fat is awkward when it takes a long time until they are gone. There is swelling and in the swelling, it is apparently sweat. The skin is destroyed by the sweat and new skin begins to grow under the old one. If you continue to eat the vegetable fat, you get many layers of skin. If you stop eating the vegetable fat, it will, in any case, takes a long time to remove many layers of skin.

Whey and the large group of vegetable fats are thus the worst cause of food allergy.

There are then some other allergens and, you can find them with the SUPER DIET.

All the time I have had problems getting protein. I knew that you have to have meat from a bull but you cannot buy beef meat; it is mixed. It is whey which is the problem. I have tried to boil away the whey, but it is not possible to remove everything. When I was standing there at the supermarket, at the fish counter, I asked for fun: What if I should eat fish?

"You do not die of fish!" said the man behind the fish counter. I bought a pike-perch fillet and went home to eat lunch. The next day I ate another fish and felt still fine. This was relief for me, the best that has happened for a long time.

When I ate fish for the fourth time, I got eczema on my scalp. It was the same eczema, which I got from eating whey. The fish did not have rum, that time of the year so it was hard to distinguish between him and she-fish. I looked at the internet and got some advice. I boughttwo pike perch fishes and ate them, now it was clear that a food allergy sufferer can eat only the male fish.

The fish has always been a certain allergen but now only 50% of them are allergen.

After the test shows that it is only possible to eat the male fish, we have got a new allergen, the female-fish hormone to contend with.

It is here, that scientists should start researching because there is too little protein for food allergy sufferers.

These last ten years I have asked for help from four Ministers of Basic Services, two Finnish presidents, and all I have said that they must try my Super Diet because that is my proof that I am right. I have also asked the Chancellor of Justice to test whether the ministers can totally ignore me.

When all the doors were closed to me, I asked my childhood friend who was retired judge from the Supreme Court.

Is it impossible for a food allergy sufferer to get help in Finland and Sweden? Top instance is the parliament, said my friend. Do you know any parliamentarian so contact him or her.

I then sent two letters and my Super Diet to all parties and in the letters, I repeated many times, "You must try my SUPER DIET because it is the proof that I am right."

It has been ten years since I wrote my book, but I still have problems getting protein, which does not cause symptoms.

Here I reproduce the two letters I sent to each political party:

Honorable MPs   Letter 1

I am an 82, years old engineer and with food allergy. In the year 2002, allergy had worsened so I thought it was cancerous.

For two and a half years I did all possible tests and after the last test (the dot test) I got the diagnosis: You have no allergy! With addition: I can guarantee that. In the two and a half years of testing, I noticed that the doctors had no grip on food allergies, and it was useless to talk to them about food allergies. I had a skilled doctor where I live, but we never talked about food allergies.

In 2004, my skin began to come off from three fingers and it was worrying.

I now started researching soybean because it was a known allergen and pork for soy to gain weight. It was difficult to find food without pork meat, but in the end, I succeeded, and the skin stopped loosening.

The blood sink was now 11 mm against 20 mm earlier. It was a great relief.

My doctor then was no "besser-wisser" but he knew that food allergy was not his brave number. He said to me: You should change environment. I moved to Spain and there it was better to find protein that does not give eczema.

In late summer 2008, I baked buns to find out what it is with the bread which I liked so much.

The buns were good but late at night I had the throat swollen, so I had to inhale cortisone, in order to sleep. This was the last bread that I ate, and it was also the answer that vegetable fat cannot be eaten if you have food allergies.

What does a person with food allergy get when he eats the Super Diet:

1 / An athlete gets about 20% more strength and now competes completely healthy.

2 / Potency does not go more up and down when the blood is free from Fibrinogen.

3 / Sleep requirement is only 7 hours. It was earlier 9 hours and I was always tired.

4 / Eczema in the scalp, neck, face, and chest is no longer activated but they begin to heal.

All this, the food allergies sufferers have neglected for 10 years when those who should have helped have not even bothered to read my Super Diet. A narcissist refuses to read a proof that he/she knew beforehand that he/she is right.

I have written the book in Swedish, Finnish, English, German and the Swedish and Finnish book has been on the Internet. I accuse: Minister Risikko, Minister Gusenina Rickardson, Minister Huovinen and Minister Saarikko and the presidents Halonen and Niinistö for not having understood the seriousness and weight of the matter.

How many food allergy sufferers have not died prematurely just because the ministers and presidents are not sufficiently responsible and competent?

When a food allergy sufferer comes becomes 55 or 60, allergy has been exacerbated so that he/she cannot sleep when the throat is swollen since it is impossible to swallow.

When I have requested that: You must test my Super diet, then the Minister replies that, thank you for giving us knowledge.

In 2008, when I first sent the e-mail to the female Minister that states: I can save 10 to 15 million euros a year with my Super Diet, so the minister's secretary replied by teaching me child-food allergy. This food allergy test, which has been used in Finland has cost, in these 10 years, about 100 million euro of the taxpayer's money, to no avail.

The only thing that I have requested from three governments, two presidents and two judiciaries is:

Test my SUPER DIET. The Parliament shall now ensure that my Super diet is tested directly, and the professors stay outside.

Letter 2, 28.05.2019
Honorable MPs

In this letter I asked that the Parliament to explain the reason why 275,000 food allergy sufferers have been waiting for 11 years to get help, despite the fact, that there has been evidence that the food allergy problem has been solved. There must be something wrong in the form of government when this can happen.

The Parliament had lively discussions when the aging care had gone a little wrong. Food allergy worsens when DNA falls and is difficult when a person is 55 to 60 years old.

When the blood sink is 20mm and the throat so swollen that it is not possible to swallow so how many have not received an early death during these 10 years.

I am 82 years old and do not think I would have lived this long if I had not solved the food allergy cause already at 70 years old. Finland's allergy professorshave been silent as "piss in the socks" during these 10 years. How to interpret this silence?

This Parliament must investigate very carefully because it is almost criminal. I have lost a lot of money and I have had difficulty when I started helping food allergy sufferers.

A lot of my pension time was wasted. I lived these 10 years as Solzhenitsyn in Stalin's Russia. When I tried to get the English book to be read by Oxford University, I was told that the professors reasoned: We do not believe that you are so stubborn in Finland that you do not help your own citizens.

This year's Nobel Prize went to one that said, it could help thousands of people.

My Super diet gives a healthy life to 550 million food allergy sufferers in the world.

www.ingramcontent.com/pod-product-compliance
Lightning Source LLC
Chambersburg PA
CBHW061628130726

47996CB00003B/1176